Coffee
EXPERIENCE

50 DELICIOUS COFFEE RECIPES AND MORE!

CELESTE JARABESE

TABLE OF CONTENTS

INTRODUCTION

COFFEE....

We are all drawn to its distinct flavor and aroma.

Coffee is considered one of the most popular beverages of all time. Aside from tea, coffee is undeniably one of life's ultimate pleasures.

In culinary, coffee is used to flavor cakes, pastries, sauces, and ice cream. It also has health-promoting benefits as it can enhance our cognitive function and stimulate our senses to become more attentive and alert.

Drinking coffee doesn't only bring comfort, but it can also promote optimum health when taken in moderation. Like tea and chocolate, coffee is an excellent source of antioxidants that can prevent the signs of aging, and it also has the ability to fight against degenerative diseases.

Among the most popular social drinks, coffee is a better alternative because it contains very minimal calories compared to regular sodas, sweetened juices, and alcoholic beverages. Just be careful about what goes into your coffee because sugar, milk, and cream can add to your daily calories. So, if you still want to enjoy your coffee without compromising your weight, try to keep these at a minimum.

This recipe book offers a wonderful collection of coffee recipes and helpful tips to guide you in creating that perfect coffee blend.

Thank you for purchasing this book, and I hope you'll enjoy all the recipes here!

With the help of this cookbook, even people suffering from health issues like heart disease, hypertension, or obesity, can now enjoy great tasting meals without having to worry about their blood cholesterol levels or fat intake. They can now include air-fried foods as a part of their healthy diet.

Sounds good, right? So, let's get started!

TIPS IN MAKING THE PERFECT COFFEE

- To make your coffee experience more pleasurable, here are some tips to guide you in creating that perfect coffee blend:

- Always buy fresh roasted and quality coffee beans. Keep them away from bright light and exposure to oxygen.

- If you want to retain its freshness and aroma, your coffee should be stored in a cool, dark, and dry place in an air-tight sealed container. NO to refrigerating or freezing of coffee beans because it can lose its delicate taste and aroma.

- Store whole coffee beans. Grinding your coffee ahead of time can lose its freshness and flavor. That is why it is best to grind them just before brewing.

- Brew your coffee with a clean paper filter. Use oxygen-bleached or dioxin-free paper filters. These can help maximize the flavor of your coffee.

- Use bottled spring water in brewing your coffee. Do not use tap water with chlorine or softened water.

- When brewing coffee, follow the recommended coffee and water ratio. Water temperature is equally important; it should be 200 F.

- Reheating, boiling, or using a warmer for a more extended period can lose the pleasant flavor and aroma of your coffee.

- Keep all your equipment clean; they should be free from oily deposits and mineral build-ups.

- When making iced coffee beverages, use coffee ice cubes made of brewed coffee instead of plain ice cubes made of water. It will give you better results.

- When making hot coffee, preheat your cup or mug as it will lengthen the time that your coffee stays warm.

HOT

Coffee

RECIPES

ORANGE-KISSED BLACK COFFEE

Preparation Time	Total Time	Yield
5 minutes	5 minutes	1 serving

INGREDIENTS

- 1 cup (250 ml) freshly brewed coffee
- 1 fl. oz. (30 ml) orange liqueur
- 1 tsp. (5 g) brown sugar (optional)
- 1/4 tsp. (0.5 g) nutmeg

METHOD

- In a serving cup, combine the brewed coffee, orange liqueur, brown sugar, and nutmeg. Stir well.
- Serve immediately and enjoy.

NUTRITIONAL INFORMATION

Energy	Fat	Carbohydrates	Protein	Sodium
78 kcal	0.3 g	3.2 g	0.3 g	6 mg

CREAMY CHOCOLATE MACCHIATO

Preparation Time	Total Time	Yield
5 minutes	5 minutes	1 serving

INGREDIENTS

- 3/4 cup (185 ml) skim milk
- 1 shot (30 ml) espresso
- 1 oz. (30 g) chocolate syrup
- 2 tsp. (5 g) cocoa powder

METHOD

- Heat the milk on the stove until it almost reaches a boil. Using a wire whisk or beater, briskly whisk to make a foam.
- In a serving glass or cup, mix together the espresso, chocolate syrup, and cocoa powder.
- Pour the milk, holding back the foam. Let milk settle at the bottom.
- Then, spoon the foam over coffee.
- Serve immediately and enjoy.

NUTRITIONAL INFORMATION

Energy	Fat	Carbohydrates	Protein	Sodium
128 kcal	0.7 g	23.2 g	7.1 g	116 mg

BLACK COFFEE WITH AMARETTO

Preparation Time	Total Time	Yield
5 minutes	5 minutes	1 serving

INGREDIENTS

- 1 cup (250 ml) freshly brewed coffee
- 1 fl. oz. (30 ml) amaretto liqueur
- 1 tsp. (5 g) brown sugar (optional)

METHOD

- In a serving cup, combine the brewed coffee, amaretto liqueur, and brown sugar. Stir well.
- Serve immediately and enjoy.

NUTRITIONAL INFORMATION

Energy	Fat	Carbohydrates	Protein	Sodium
24 kcal	0.1 g	5.6 g	0.3 g	7 mg

COFFEE VANILLA PUMPKIN PIE

Preparation Time	Total Time	Yield
5 minutes	5 minutes	1 serving

INGREDIENTS

- 3/4 cup (185 ml) strong brewed coffee
- 1 Tbsp. (20 g) pumpkin puree
- 1 Tbsp. (15 g) whipped cream
- 1 Tbsp. (20 ml) vanilla-flavored syrup
- 1/4 tsp. (0.5 g) cinnamon, ground
- 1/4 tsp. (0.5 g) nutmeg, ground

METHOD

- Combine the coffee, pumpkin puree, whipped cream, vanilla syrup, cinnamon, and nutmeg. Stir well.
- Serve immediately and enjoy.

NUTRITIONAL INFORMATION

Energy	Fat	Carbohydrates	Protein	Sodium
95 kcal	4.9 g	12.9 g	0.8 g	12 mg

PEPPERMINT BLACK COFFEE

Preparation Time	Total Time	Yield
5 minutes	5 minutes	1 serving

INGREDIENTS

- 1 cup (250 ml) freshly brewed coffee
- 1 drop (1 ml) peppermint extract
- 1 tsp. (5 g) brown sugar

METHOD

- In a serving cup, combine the brewed coffee, peppermint extract, and brown sugar. Stir well.
- Serve immediately and enjoy.

NUTRITIONAL INFORMATION

Energy	Fat	Carbohydrates	Protein	Sodium
17 kcal	0.1 g	4.0 g	0.3 g	5 mg

CHOCO MALT CAPPUCCINO

Preparation Time	Total Time	Yield
5 minutes	5 minutes	1 serving

INGREDIENTS

- 3/4 cup (185 ml) skim milk
- 1 shot (30 ml) espresso
- 1 Tbsp. (7 g) chocolate malt powder
- 1/4 tsp. (0.5 g) cinnamon, ground

METHOD

- Heat the milk on the stove until it almost reaches a boil. Whisk briskly using a wire whisk to produce foam.
- In a serving glass or cup, mix together the espresso, chocolate malt powder, and cinnamon.
- Pour the milk and then add the foam.
- Serve immediately and enjoy.

NUTRITIONAL INFORMATION

Energy	Fat	Carbohydrates	Protein	Sodium
156 kcal	1.0 g	27.7 g	7.1 g	142 mg

SWEET BLACK COFFEE MEXICAN-STYLE

Preparation Time	Total Time	Yield
5 minutes	5 minutes	1 serving

INGREDIENTS

- 1 cup (250 ml) freshly brewed strong coffee
- 1 tsp. (5 g) molasses
- 1 tsp. (5 g) brown sugar
- Pinch of ground cinnamon
- Pinch of nutmeg

METHOD

- In a serving cup, combine the brewed coffee, molasses, brown sugar, cinnamon, and nutmeg. Stir well.
- Serve immediately and enjoy.

NUTRITIONAL INFORMATION

Energy	Fat	Carbohydrates	Protein	Sodium
34 kcal	1.0 g	8.2 g	0.3 g	8 mg

MINTY CAFÉ MOCHA

Preparation Time	Total Time	Yield
5 minutes	5 minutes	1 serving

INGREDIENTS

- 3/4 cup (185 ml) skim milk
- 1 shot (30 ml) espresso
- 1 Tbsp. (20 g) chocolate syrup
- 1 tsp. (2.5 g) cocoa powder
- 1 drop (1 ml) peppermint extract

METHOD

- Heat the milk on the stove until it almost reaches a boil. Whisk briskly using a wire whisk to make a foam.
- In a serving cup, mix together the espresso, chocolate syrup, cocoa powder, and mint.
- Pour the milk and foam over coffee mixture.
- Serve immediately and enjoy.

NUTRITIONAL INFORMATION

Energy	Fat	Carbohydrates	Protein	Sodium
137 kcal	0.5 g	22.5 g	6.8 g	116 mg

CARDAMOM-SPICED BLACK COFFEE

Preparation Time	Total Time	Yield
5 minutes	5 minutes	1 serving

INGREDIENTS

- 1 cup (250 ml) freshly brewed coffee
- 1 tsp. (5 g) brown sugar (optional)
- 1/4 tsp. (0.5 g) cardamom, ground

METHOD

- In a serving cup, combine the brewed coffee, brown sugar, and cardamom. Stir well.
- Serve immediately and enjoy.

NUTRITIONAL INFORMATION

Energy	Fat	Carbohydrates	Protein	Sodium
15 kcal	0.1 g	3.3 g	0.3 g	6 mg

ALMOND CHOCO COFFEE

Preparation Time	Total Time	Yield
5 minutes	5 minutes	1 serving

INGREDIENTS

- 3/4 cup (185 ml) almond milk
- 1 shot (30 ml) espresso
- 1 Tbsp. (15 ml) amaretto almond liqueur
- 1 Tbsp. (20 ml) chocolate syrup

METHOD

- In a small saucepan, bring almond milk to a simmer. Remove from heat. Whisk briskly using a wire whisk to produce foam or if you have, use a milk frother.
- In a serving cup, mix together the espresso, almond milk amaretto liqueur, and chocolate syrup.
- Pour the milk and foam over coffee.
- Serve immediately and enjoy.

NUTRITIONAL INFORMATION

Energy	Fat	Carbohydrates	Protein	Sodium
137 kcal	0.5 g	22.5 g	6.8 g	116 mg

BLACK HAZELNUT COFFEE WITH MAPLE

Preparation Time	Total Time	Yield
5 minutes	5 minutes	1 serving

INGREDIENTS

- 1 cup (250 ml) strong brewed coffee
- 1 Tbsp. (20 ml) hazelnut syrup
- 1 tsp. (7 ml) maple syrup

METHOD

- In a serving cup, combine the brewed coffee, hazelnut syrup, and maple syrup. Stir well.
- Serve immediately and enjoy.

NUTRITIONAL INFORMATION

Energy	Fat	Carbohydrates	Protein	Sodium
49 kcal	2.9 g	5.3 g	1 g	5 mg

CINNAMON-SPICED CAFÉ AMERICANO

Preparation Time	Total Time	Yield
5 minutes	5 minutes	1 serving

INGREDIENTS

- 3/4 cup (185 ml) hot water
- 1 oz. (30 ml) espresso
- 1/4 tsp. cinnamon, ground
- Brown sugar, to taste (optional)

METHOD

- Combine the hot water, espresso, and cinnamon in a serving cup. Stir well.
- Sweeten with brown sugar if desired.
- Serve immediately and enjoy.

NUTRITIONAL INFORMATION

Energy	Fat	Carbohydrates	Protein	Sodium
17 kcal	0 g	4.5 g	0.1 g	9 mg

CAFE AU LAIT WITH HONEY

Preparation Time	Total Time	Yield
5 minutes	5 minutes	1 serving

INGREDIENTS

- 2/3 cup (165 ml) strong brewed coffee
- 1/3 cup (85 ml) heated or steamed milk
- 1 tsp. (7 ml) honey

METHOD

- Combine the brewed coffee, heated milk, and honey in a serving cup. Stir well.
- Serve immediately and enjoy.

NUTRITIONAL INFORMATION

Energy	Fat	Carbohydrates	Protein	Sodium
83 kcal	2.5 g	11.8 g	4.2 g	60 mg

COFFEE VANILLA CREAM

Preparation Time	Total Time	Yield
5 minutes	5 minutes	1 serving

INGREDIENTS

- 1 cup (250 ml) freshly brewed coffee
- 1 Tbsp. (15 g) heavy cream
- 1 tsp. (5 g) raw sugar
- 1/4 tsp. pure vanilla extract

METHOD

- In a serving cup, combine the brewed coffee, heavy cream, raw sugar, and vanilla extract. Stir well.
- Serve immediately and enjoy.

NUTRITIONAL INFORMATION

Energy	Fat	Carbohydrates	Protein	Sodium
72 kcal	5.6 g	4.6 g	0.6 g	11 mg

SWEET ALMOND COFFEE

Preparation Time	Total Time	Yield
5 minutes	5 minutes	1 serving

INGREDIENTS

- 1/2 cup (185 ml) hot water
- 1 shot (30 ml) espresso
- 2 oz. (60 ml) almond milk
- 1/4 tsp. almond extract
- 1 tsp. (5 g) brown sugar

METHOD

- In a serving cup, combine the hot water, espresso, almond milk, almond extract, and brown sugar. Stir well.
- Serve immediately and enjoy.

NUTRITIONAL INFORMATION

Energy	Fat	Carbohydrates	Protein	Sodium
22 kcal	0.3 g	4.6 g	0.2 g	29 mg

BROWN MOCHA ALMOND

Preparation Time	Total Time	Yield
5 minutes	5 minutes	1 serving

INGREDIENTS

- 3/4 cup (185 ml) almond milk
- 1 shot (30 ml) espresso
- 2 tsp. (5 g) cocoa powder
- 1 tsp. (5 g) brown sugar

METHOD

- Heat the almond milk on the stove until it almost reaches a boil. Whisk briskly using a wire whisk to produce foam.
- In a serving cup, mix together the espresso, cocoa powder, and sugar.
- Stir in heated milk and foam.
- Serve immediately and enjoy.

NUTRITIONAL INFORMATION

Energy	Fat	Carbohydrates	Protein	Sodium
47 kcal	2.2 g	6.7 g	1.3 g	119 mg

HOT MOCHACCINO RECIPE

Preparation Time	Total Time	Yield
5 minutes	5 minutes	1 serving

INGREDIENTS

- 3/4 cup (185 ml) skim milk
- 1 shot (30 ml) espresso
- 1 Tbsp. (20 ml) chocolate syrup
- 1/4 tsp. cinnamon, ground

METHOD

- Heat the skim milk on the stove until it almost reaches a boil. Whisk briskly using a wire whisk to produce foam.
- In a serving cup, mix together the espresso and chocolate syrup.
- Pour the milk, holding back the foam. Then, allow the milk to settle at the bottom.
- Spoon foam over coffee and then sprinkle with cinnamon.
- Serve immediately and enjoy.

NUTRITIONAL INFORMATION

Energy	Fat	Carbohydrates	Protein	Sodium
122 kcal	0.2 g	21.7 g	6.5 g	115 mg

CREAMED BELGIAN COFFEE

Preparation Time	Total Time	Yield
5 minutes	5 minutes	1 serving

INGREDIENTS

- 2 shots (60 ml) espresso
- 1 fl. oz. (30 ml) Belgian cookie syrup
- 2 oz. (60 g) whipped cream
- Dark chocolate, grated

METHOD

- In a serving cup, stir together the espresso and Belgian cookie syrup.
- Top with whipped cream and sprinkle with grated dark chocolate.
- Serve immediately and enjoy.

NUTRITIONAL INFORMATION

Energy	Fat	Carbohydrates	Protein	Sodium
188 kcal	17.4 g	1.9 g	1.1 g	29 mg

CAFÉ CHOCO LATTE RECIPE

Preparation Time	Total Time	Yield
5 minutes	5 minutes	1 serving

INGREDIENTS

- 3/4 cup (185 ml) whole milk
- 2 shots (60 ml) espresso
- 2 Tbsp. (40 ml) chocolate syrup, divided

METHOD

- Heat the milk on the stove until it almost reaches a boil. Whisk briskly using a wire whisk to produce foam or you can also use a milk frother if you have.
- In a serving cup, mix together the espresso and 1 tablespoon chocolate syrup.
- Pour the milk with foam in the center. Drizzle with remaining chocolate syrup in a circular motion.
- Serve immediately and enjoy.

NUTRITIONAL INFORMATION

Energy	Fat	Carbohydrates	Protein	Sodium
216 kcal	6.4 g	32.7 g	6.8 g	109 mg

CREAMY COFFEE CARAMEL

Preparation Time	Total Time	Yield
5 minutes	5 minutes	1 serving

INGREDIENTS

- 3/4 cup (185 ml) skim milk
- 2 shots (60 ml) espresso
- 2 Tbsp. (40 ml) caramel sauce

METHOD

- Heat the milk on the stove until it almost reaches a boil. Whisk briskly using a wire whisk to produce foam or you can also use a milk frother if you have.
- In a serving cup, mix together the espresso and 1 tablespoon caramel sauce.
- Pour the milk and foam. Then, drizzle with remaining caramel sauce.
- Serve immediately and enjoy.

NUTRITIONAL INFORMATION

Energy	Fat	Carbohydrates	Protein	Sodium
172 kcal	0 g	36.0 g	6.7 g	249 mg

IRISH CREAM COFFEE

Preparation Time	Total Time	Yield
5 minutes	5 minutes	1 serving

INGREDIENTS

- 1 cup (250 ml) freshly brewed coffee
- 1 fl. oz. (30 ml) Irish cream liqueur
- 1 tsp. (5 g) brown sugar
- Whipped cream, to serve

METHOD

- In a serving cup, combine the brewed coffee, Irish cream liqueur, and brown sugar. Stir well.
- Top with some whipped cream.
- Serve immediately and enjoy.

NUTRITIONAL INFORMATION

Energy	Fat	Carbohydrates	Protein	Sodium
149 kcal	8.3 g	10.4 g	1.5 g	33 mg

FRENCH VANILLA MOCHA

Preparation Time	Total Time	Yield
5 minutes	5 minutes	1 serving

INGREDIENTS

- 3/4 cup (185 ml) skim milk
- 2 shots (60 ml) espresso
- 1 fl. oz. (30 ml) French vanilla syrup
- 1 tsp. (2.5 g) cocoa powder

METHOD

- Heat the milk on the stove until it almost reaches a boil. Whisk briskly using a wire whisk to produce foam or use a milk frother if you have.
- In a serving cup, mix together the espresso, French vanilla syrup, and cocoa powder.
- Pour the milk, holding back the foam. Allow milk to settle at the bottom.
- Spoon foam over coffee.
- Serve immediately and enjoy.

NUTRITIONAL INFORMATION

Energy	Fat	Carbohydrates	Protein	Sodium
122 kcal	0.2 g	23.0 g	6.4 g	105 mg

MALTED CAPPUCCINO

Preparation Time	Total Time	Yield
5 minutes	5 minutes	1 servings

INGREDIENTS

- 3/4 cup (185 ml) whole milk
- 2 shots (60 ml) espresso
- 1 Tbsp. (7 g) chocolate malt powder
- 1 tsp. (5 g) muscovado or raw sugar
- 1/4 tsp. (0.5 g) cinnamon, ground

METHOD

- Heat the whole milk on the stove until it almost reaches a boil. Whisk briskly using a wire whisk to produce foam or use a milk frother if you have.
- In a serving cup, mix together espresso, chocolate malt powder, and muscovado.
- Pour the milk, holding back the foam. Allow milk to settle at the bottom.
- Spoon foam over coffee. Sprinkle with cinnamon.
- Serve immediately and enjoy.

NUTRITIONAL INFORMATION

Energy	Fat	Carbohydrates	Protein	Sodium
214 kcal	7.0 g	31.0 g	7.1 g	122 mg

GINGERBREAD SPICED HOLIDAY COFFEE

Preparation Time	Total Time	Yield
5 minutes	5 minutes	1 serving

INGREDIENTS

- 1 cup (250 ml) freshly brewed coffee
- 1 oz. (30 ml) gingerbread spice syrup
- 1 ½ oz. (45 g) whipped cream
- Nutmeg, to serve
- Gingerbread cookie crumbs, to serve

METHOD

- In a serving cup, combine the brewed coffee and gingerbread spice syrup.
- Top with whipped cream and sprinkle with nutmeg and gingerbread cookie crumbs.
- Serve immediately and enjoy.

NUTRITIONAL INFORMATION

Energy	Fat	Carbohydrates	Protein	Sodium
210 calories	13.4 g	20.8 g	1.2 g	22 mg

COFFEE COCONUT WITH HONEY

Preparation Time	Total Time	Yield
5 minutes	5 minutes	1 serving

INGREDIENTS

- 1 cup (250 ml) strong brewed coffee
- 1 oz. (30 g) coconut cream
- 1 tsp. (7 ml) honey

METHOD

- In a serving cup, combine the brewed coffee, coconut cream, and honey. Stir well.
- Serve immediately and enjoy.

NUTRITIONAL INFORMATION

Energy	Fat	Carbohydrates	Protein	Sodium
108 kcal	6.8 g	13.3 g	0.7 g	5 mg

RASPBERRY CREAM COFFEE

Preparation Time	Total Time	Yield
5 minutes	5 minutes	1 serving

INGREDIENTS

- 3/4 cup (185 ml) skim milk
- 2 shots (60 ml) espresso
- 1 fl. oz. (30 ml) raspberry syrup

METHOD

- Heat the whole milk on the stove until it almost reaches a boil. Whisk briskly with a wire whisk to produce foam or use a milk frother if you have.
- In a serving cup, mix together the espresso and raspberry syrup.
- Pour the milk, holding back the foam. Allow milk to settle at the bottom.
- Spoon foam over coffee.
- Serve immediately and enjoy.

NUTRITIONAL INFORMATION

Energy	Fat	Carbohydrates	Protein	Sodium
149 kcal	0.1 g	29.0 g	6.1 g	106 mg

CAFÉ CON LECHE RECIPE

Preparation Time	Total Time	Yield
5 minutes	5 minutes	1 serving

INGREDIENTS

- 3/4 cup (185 ml) whole milk, heated or steamed
- 2 shots (60 ml) espresso
- 1 tsp. (7 ml) heavy cream
- 2 tsp. (10 g) raw sugar

METHOD

- In a serving cup, combine the heated milk, espresso, cream, and raw sugar. Stir well.
- Serve immediately and enjoy.

NUTRITIONAL INFORMATION

Energy	Fat	Carbohydrates	Protein	Sodium
158 kcal	7.8 g	16.4 g	6.1 g	84 mg

ICED COFFEE
recipes

CREAMY CARAMEL MOCHA

Preparation Time	Total Time	Yield
5 minutes	5 minutes	1 serving

INGREDIENTS

- 2 shots (60 ml) espresso
- 4 fl. oz. (125 ml) skim milk
- 1 Tbsp. (20 ml) chocolate syrup
- 1 Tbsp. (20 ml) caramel syrup
- 1 Tbsp. (20 ml) caramel sauce
- Whipped cream, to serve
- 6-8 ice cubes

METHOD

- Fill half of the shaker bottle with ice cubes. Add the espresso, milk, chocolate syrup, and caramel syrup. Cover and shake to combine well.
- Pour the coffee mixture with ice into a tall glass. Top with whipped cream and then drizzle with 1 tablespoon caramel sauce.
- Serve and enjoy.

NUTRITIONAL INFORMATION

Energy	Fat	Carbohydrates	Protein	Sodium
251 kcal	4.9 g	46.3 g	4.9 g	166 mg

ICED COFFEE ALMOND JOY

Preparation Time	Total Time	Yield
5 minutes	5 minutes	1 serving

INGREDIENTS

- 2 shots (60 ml) espresso
- 3/4 cup (185 ml) almond milk
- 1 ½ oz. (45 ml) chocolate syrup
- 1/4 tsp. (0.5 g) nutmeg
- 1 tsp. (2.5 g) toasted coconut flakes
- 6-8 ice cubes

METHOD

- Fill half of the shaker bottle with ice cubes. Add the espresso, almond milk, and chocolate syrup. Cover and shake to combine well.
- Pour the coffee mixture with ice into a tall glass. Sprinkle with nutmeg and coconut flakes.
- Serve and enjoy.

NUTRITIONAL INFORMATION

Energy	Fat	Carbohydrates	Protein	Sodium
174 kcal	3.1 g	34.2 g	1.8 g	152 mg

ICED CAFÉ LATTE

Preparation Time	Total Time	Yield
5 minutes	5 minutes	1 serving

INGREDIENTS

- 2 shots (60 ml) espresso
- 3/4 cup (185 ml) low-fat milk
- 2 tsp. (10 g) brown sugar
- 6 coffee ice cubes

METHOD

- Fill half of the shaker bottle with ice cubes. Add espresso, low-fat milk, and brown sugar. Cover and shake to combine well.
- Pour the coffee mixture with ice into a tall glass.
- Serve and enjoy.

NUTRITIONAL INFORMATION

Energy	Fat	Carbohydrates	Protein	Sodium
103 kcal	1.7 g	16.5 g	5.8 g	83 mg

BANANA COFFEE AND OAT SMOOTHIE

Preparation Time	Total Time	Yield
5 minutes	5 minutes	1 serving

INGREDIENTS

- 6 fl. oz. (185 ml) low-fat milk
- 1/2 medium (120 g) banana, cut into small pieces
- 2 shots (60 ml) espresso
- 2 Tbsp. (15 g) rolled oats
- 1 Tbsp. (7 g) wheat germ
- 1 tsp. (7 g) agave nectar
- 1/4 tsp. pure vanilla extract
- 6 ice cubes
- nutmeg, to serve

METHOD

- In a blender, combine the milk, banana, espresso, rolled oats, wheat germ, agave nectar, vanilla extract, and ice cubes. Process until smooth.
- Pour the blended coffee mixture into a chilled serving glass. Sprinkle with nutmeg.
- Serve immediately and enjoy.

NUTRITIONAL INFORMATION

Energy	Fat	Carbohydrates	Protein	Sodium
264 kcal	3.5 g	50.8 g	10.8 g	85 mg

ICED HAZELNUT COFFEE

Preparation Time	Total Time	Yield
5 minutes	5 minutes	1 serving

INGREDIENTS

- 3/4 cup (185 ml) strong brewed coffee
- 1/3 cup (85 ml) skim milk
- 1 ½ fl. oz. (45 ml) hazelnut syrup
- 6 coffee ice cubes

METHOD

- Fill half of the shaker bottle with coffee ice cubes. Add the brewed coffee, skim milk, and hazelnut syrup. Cover and shake to combine well.
- Pour the coffee mixture with ice into a tall glass.
- Serve and enjoy.

NUTRITIONAL INFORMATION

Energy	Fat	Carbohydrates	Protein	Sodium
112 kcal	0 g	23.0 g	2.9 g	47 mg

SUGAR-FREE ALMOND COFFEE

Preparation Time	Total Time	Yield
5 minutes	5 minutes	1 serving

INGREDIENTS

- 1 cup (250 ml) strong brewed coffee
- 1/4 cup (60 ml) almond milk, unsweetened
- Stevia, to taste
- 6 ice cubes

METHOD

- Fill half of the shaker bottle with ice cubes. Add the brewed coffee, almond milk, and stevia. Cover and shake to combine well.
- Pour the coffee mixture with ice into a tall glass.
- Serve immediately and enjoy.

NUTRITIONAL INFORMATION

Energy	Fat	Carbohydrates	Protein	Sodium
12 kcal	0.9 g	2.3 g	0.5 g	53 mg

LOW-FAT MOCHA CREAM SHAKE

Preparation Time	Total Time	Yield
5 minutes	5 minutes	1 serving

INGREDIENTS

- 2/3 cup (165 ml) strong brewed coffee, cooled
- 1/3 cup (85 ml) almond milk
- 1 scoop (60 g) fat-free chocolate ice cream
- 6 coffee ice cubes
- Fat-free whipped cream, to serve
- Dark chocolate syrup, to serve

METHOD

- In a blender, combine the brewed coffee, almond milk, chocolate ice cream, and coffee ice cubes. Process until smooth.
- Pour the blended coffee mixture into a chilled glass. Top with whipped cream and then drizzle with dark chocolate syrup.
- Serve immediately and enjoy.

NUTRITIONAL INFORMATION

Energy	Fat	Carbohydrates	Protein	Sodium
198 kcal	5.7 g	34.0 g	4.2 g	122 mg

DARK CHOCO VANILLA AND COFFEE SMOOTHIE

Preparation Time	Total Time	Yield
5 minutes	5 minutes	1 serving

INGREDIENTS

- 2/3 cup (165 ml) strong brewed coffee, cooled
- 1/3 cup (85 ml) skim milk
- 1 scoop (60 g) fat-free vanilla ice cream
- 1 Tbsp. (20 ml) dark chocolate syrup
- 6 coffee ice cubes

METHOD

- In a blender, combine the brewed coffee, skim milk, vanilla ice cream, dark chocolate syrup, and coffee ice cubes. Process until smooth.
- Pour the blended coffee mixture into a chilled glass.
- Serve immediately and enjoy.

NUTRITIONAL INFORMATION

Energy	Fat	Carbohydrates	Protein	Sodium
221 kcal	7.2 g	32.2 g	5.6 g	113 mg

SPICED MOCHA SHAKE

Preparation Time	Total Time	Yield
5 minutes	5 minutes	1 serving

INGREDIENTS

- 2 shots (60 ml) espresso
- 1/3 cup (85 ml) low-fat milk
- 1 Tbsp. (20 ml) chocolate syrup
- 2 tsp. (5 g) cocoa powder
- 1/4 tsp. cinnamon, ground
- 6 coffee ice cubes

METHOD

- In a high-speed blender, combine the espresso, low-fat milk, chocolate syrup, cocoa powder, and cinnamon. Process until combined well.
- Add the ice cubes and blend further 30 seconds or until smooth.
- Pour the blended coffee mixture into a chilled glass. Garnish with coffee beans, if desired.
- Serve immediately and enjoy.

NUTRITIONAL INFORMATION

Energy	Fat	Carbohydrates	Protein	Sodium
97 kcal	1.5 g	18.7 g	3.9 g	3.9 mg

PEPPERMINT MOCHA FRAPPE

Preparation Time	Total Time	Yield
5 minutes	5 minutes	1 serving

INGREDIENTS

- 3/4 cup (185 ml) strong brewed coffee
- 1/3 cup (85 ml) skim milk
- 1 fl. oz. (30 ml) chocolate syrup
- 1 fl. oz. (30 ml) peppermint syrup
- 6 coffee ice cubes

METHOD

- In a high-speed blender, combine the brewed coffee, skim milk, chocolate syrup, peppermint syrup, and coffee ice cubes. Process until smooth.
- Pour the blended coffee mixture into a chilled glass.
- Serve immediately and enjoy.

NUTRITIONAL INFORMATION

Energy	Fat	Carbohydrates	Protein	Sodium
181 kcal	0.4 g	39.5 g	3.5 g	72 mg

RASPBERRY CHOCO COFFEE SHAKE

Preparation Time	Total Time	Yield
5 minutes	5 minutes	1 serving

INGREDIENTS

- 3/4 cup (185 ml) strong brewed coffee
- 1/3 cup (85 ml) skim milk
- 1 fl. oz. (30 ml) raspberry syrup
- 1 fl. oz. (30 ml) chocolate syrup
- 6 coffee ice cubes
- Cocoa powder, to serve

METHOD

- In a high-speed blender, combine the brewed coffee, skim milk, raspberry syrup, chocolate syrup, and coffee ice cubes.
- Pour the blended coffee mixture into a chilled glass. Sprinkle with some cocoa powder.
- Serve immediately and enjoy.

NUTRITIONAL INFORMATION

Energy	Fat	Carbohydrates	Protein	Sodium
157 calories	0 g	35.0 g	2.9 g	117 mg

ICED MACADAMIA MOCHA

Preparation Time	Total Time	Yield
5 minutes	5 minutes	1 serving

INGREDIENTS

- 3/4 cup (185 ml) strong brewed coffee
- 1/4 cup (60 ml) low-fat milk
- 1 fl. oz. (30 ml) macadamia nut syrup, sugar-free
- 1 fl. oz. (30 ml) white crème de cacao
- 6 ice cubes

METHOD

- Fill half of the shaker bottle with ice cubes. Add the brewed coffee, milk, macadamia nut syrup, and white crème de cacao. Cover and shake to combine well.
- Pour the coffee mixture with ice into a tall glass.
- Serve immediately and enjoy.

NUTRITIONAL INFORMATION

Energy	Fat	Carbohydrates	Protein	Sodium
46 kcal	0.8 g	6.6 g	2.9 g	40 mg

SPICED IRISH CREAM COFFEE FRAPPE

Preparation Time	Total Time	Yield
5 minutes	5 minutes	1 serving

INGREDIENTS

- 3/4 cup (185 ml) strong brewed coffee, cooled
- 1/3 cup (85 ml) low-fat milk
- 1 fl. oz. (30 ml) Irish cream liqueur
- 2 tsp. (10 g) brown sugar
- 1/4 tsp. (0.5 g) ground cinnamon
- 6 coffee ice cubes
- Whipped cream, to serve
- Ground nutmeg, to serve

METHOD

- In a high-speed blender, combine the brewed coffee, Irish cream liqueur, milk, brown sugar, cinnamon, and coffee ice cubes.
- Pour the blended coffee mixture into a chilled glass. Top with whipped cream and then sprinkle with some ground nutmeg.
- Serve immediately and enjoy.

NUTRITIONAL INFORMATION

Energy	Fat	Carbohydrates	Protein	Sodium
198 kcal	9.3 g	18.1 g	4.2 g	68 mg

ICED CAFÉ LATTE WITH MAPLE

Preparation Time	Total Time	Yield
5 minutes	5 minutes	1 serving

INGREDIENTS

- 2 shots (60 ml) espresso
- 4 oz. (125 ml) whole milk
- 1 Tbsp. (20 ml) maple syrup
- 6 ice cubes

METHOD

- Fill half of the shaker bottle with coffee ice cubes. Add the espresso, milk, and maple syrup. Cover and shake to combine well.
- Pour the coffee mixture with ice into a tall glass.
- Serve immediately and enjoy.

NUTRITIONAL INFORMATION

Energy	Fat	Carbohydrates	Protein	Sodium
155 kcal	5.6 g	21.1 g	5.6 g	78 mg

MOCHA CARAMEL FRAPPE

Preparation Time	Total Time	Yield
5 minutes	5 minutes	1 serving

INGREDIENTS

- 3/4 cup (185 ml) strong brewed coffee, cooled
- 1/3 cup (85 ml) low-fat milk
- 1 fl. oz. (30 ml) caramel syrup, sugar-free
- 1 fl. oz. (30 ml) white crème de cacao
- 6 coffee ice cubes
- Whipped cream, to serve
- Caramel sauce or chocolate sauce, to serve

METHOD

- In a high-speed blender, combine the brewed coffee, low-fat milk, caramel syrup, white crème de cacao, and coffee ice cubes. Process until smooth.
- Pour the blended coffee mixture into a chilled glass. Top with whipped cream and drizzle with some caramel or chocolate sauce.
- Serve immediately and enjoy.

NUTRITIONAL INFORMATION

Energy	Fat	Carbohydrates	Protein	Sodium
131 kcal	5.5 g	18 g	3.6 g	126 mg

ICE CREAM CHOCO JAVA

Preparation Time	Total Time	Yield
5 minutes	5 minutes	1 serving

INGREDIENTS

- 2/3 cup (165 ml) strong brewed coffee
- 1/3 cup (85 ml) skim milk
- 1 fl. oz. (30 ml) hazelnut syrup
- 1/2 tsp. (1 g) cinnamon, ground
- 1 scoop (60 g) fat-free chocolate ice cream
- Coffee ice cubes

METHOD

- Fill half of the shaker bottle with coffee ice cubes. Add the brewed coffee, skim milk, hazelnut syrup, and cinnamon. Cover and shake to combine well.
- Pour the coffee mixture with ice into a tall glass. Top with a scoop of fat-free chocolate ice cream.
- Serve and enjoy.

NUTRITIONAL INFORMATION

Energy	Fat	Carbohydrates	Protein	Sodium
214 Kcal	1.5 g	41.9 g	7.9 g	107 mg

EASY NUTELLA FRAPPE

Preparation Time	Total Time	Yield
5 minutes	5 minutes	1 serving

INGREDIENTS

- 3/4 cup (185 ml) strong brewed coffee, cooled
- 1/3 cup (85 ml) skim milk
- 1 oz. (30 g) chocolate-hazelnut spread (Nutella)
- 1 fl. oz. (30 ml) mocha syrup, sugar-free
- 6 coffee ice cubes
- Whipped cream, to serve
- Chocolate syrup, to serve

METHOD

- In a high-speed blender, combine the brewed coffee, milk, Nutella, mocha syrup, and coffee ice cubes. Process until smooth.
- Pour the blended coffee mixture into a chilled glass. Top with some whipped cream and then drizzle with chocolate syrup.
- Serve immediately and enjoy.

NUTRITIONAL INFORMATION

Energy	Fat	Carbohydrates	Protein	Sodium
300 kcal	16.2 g	30.5 g	7.2 g	67 mg

ICED VIETNAMESE COFFEE

Preparation Time	Total Time	Yield
5 minutes	5 minutes	1 serving

INGREDIENTS

- 2 shots (60 ml) espresso
- 3 fl. oz. (90 ml) low-fat milk
- 1 Tbsp. (20 g) condensed milk
- 6 ice cubes

METHOD

- Fill half of the shaker bottle with ice cubes. Add the espresso, low-fat milk, and condensed milk. Cover and shake to combine well.
- Pour the coffee mixture with ice into a tall glass.
- Serve immediately and enjoy.

NUTRITIONAL INFORMATION

Energy	Fat	Carbohydrates	Protein	Sodium
98 kcal	2.5 g	14.6 g	4.5 g	70 mg

ICED COFFEE WITH PUMPKIN SPICE

Preparation Time	Total Time	Yield
5 minutes	5 minutes	1 serving

INGREDIENTS

- 3/4 (185 ml) strong brewed coffee
- 1/3 cup (85 ml) skim milk
- 1 ½ fl. oz. (45 ml) mocha syrup
- 1/2 tsp. (1 g) pumpkin spice
- 6 coffee ice cubes
- Cinnamon, to serve

METHOD

- Fill half of the shaker bottle with coffee ice cubes. Add the brewed coffee, milk, mocha syrup, and pumpkin spice. Cover and shake to combine well.
- Pour the coffee mixture with ice into a tall glass. Sprinkle with cinnamon.
- Serve and enjoy.

NUTRITIONAL INFORMATION

Energy	Fat	Carbohydrates	Protein	Sodium
72 Kcal	0.9 g	10.6 g	4.4 g	47 mg

CHOCOLATE CHERRY ICED COFFEE

Preparation Time	Total Time	Yield
5 minutes	5 minutes	1 serving

INGREDIENTS

- 3/4 cup (185 ml) strong brewed coffee
- 1/3 cup (85 ml) skim milk
- 1 fl. oz. (30 ml) chocolate syrup
- 1 fl. oz. (30 ml) cherry juice
- 6 coffee ice cubes

METHOD

- Fill half of the shaker bottle with coffee ice cubes. Add the brewed coffee, milk, chocolate syrup, and cherry juice. Cover and shake to combine well.
- Pour the coffee mixture with ice into a tall glass.
- Serve and enjoy.

NUTRITIONAL INFORMATION

Energy	Fat	Carbohydrates	Protein	Sodium
125 kcal	0.4 g	25.8 g	3.5 g	69 mg

FROZEN CHOCOLATE MACADAMIA COFFEE

Preparation Time	Total Time	Yield
5 minutes	5 minutes	1 serving

INGREDIENTS

- 3/4 cup (185 ml) strong brewed coffee
- 1/4 cup (60 ml) low-fat milk
- 1 fl. oz. (30 ml) macadamia syrup
- 1 fl. oz. (30 ml) dark chocolate sauce
- 6 coffee ice cubes
- Dash of cocoa powder, to serve

METHOD

- In a high-speed blender, combine the brewed coffee, low-fat milk, macadamia syrup, dark chocolate sauce, and coffee ice cubes.
- Pour the blended coffee mixture into a chilled glass. Sprinkle with cocoa powder.
- Serve immediately and enjoy.

NUTRITIONAL INFORMATION

Energy	Fat	Carbohydrates	Protein	Sodium
128 kcal	1.6 g	26.3 g	3.8 g	85 mg

CHILLED BANANA CARAMEL COFFEE

Preparation Time	Total Time	Yield
5 minutes	5 minutes	1 serving

INGREDIENTS

- 2 shots (60 ml) espresso
- 4 fl. oz. (125 ml) almond milk
- 1 small (100 g) banana, cut into small pieces
- 2 Tbsp. (40 ml) caramel sauce, divided
- 6 ice cubes

METHOD

- In a high-speed blender, combine the espresso, almond milk, banana, 1 tablespoon caramel sauce, and ice cubes.
- Pour the blended coffee mixture into a chilled glass. Drizzle with remaining caramel sauce.
- Serve immediately and enjoy.

NUTRITIONAL INFORMATION

Energy	Fat	Carbohydrates	Protein	Sodium
224 kcal	2.9 g	51.1 g	2.8 g	303 mg

BONUS RECIPES

COFFEE VANILLA MILKSHAKE

Preparation Time	Total Time	Yield
5 minutes	5 minutes	1 serving

INGREDIENTS

- 2 (60 g) scoops vanilla ice cream, divided
- 2/3 cup (165 ml) skim milk
- 2 shots (60 ml) espresso, cooled
- 5-6 cubes ice

METHOD

- In a high-speed blender, combine the espresso, 1 scoop ice cream, skim milk, and ice. Process until smooth
- Pour the blended coffee mixture into a chilled glass. Top with remaining scoop of ice cream.
- Serve immediately and enjoy.

NUTRITIONAL INFORMATION

Energy	Fat	Carbohydrates	Protein	Sodium
224 kcal	2.9 g	51.1 g	2.8 g	303 mg

COFFEE FRAPPE WITH CINNAMON

Preparation Time	Total Time	Yield
5 minutes	5 minutes	2 servings

INGREDIENTS

- 1 ½ cups (375 ml) strong brewed coffee
- 3/4 cup (185 ml) cold milk
- 2 Tbsp. (30 ml) sugar-free syrup
- 1/2 tsp. (1 g) ground cinnamon
- 10 ice cubes
- Whipped cream

METHOD

- Place the brewed coffee, cold milk, sugar-free syrup, cinnamon, and ice cubes in a high-speed blender. Process until smooth.
- Pour the coffee mixture into 2 chilled tall glasses. Top with some whipped cream and sprinkle with more cinnamon if desired.
- Serve and enjoy.

NUTRITIONAL INFORMATION

Energy	Fat	Carbohydrates	Protein	Sodium
230 kcal	13.1 g	23.0 g	7.0 g	108 mg

COFFEE CHOCO HAZELNUT FRAPPE

Preparation Time	Total Time	Yield
5 minutes	5 minutes	2 servings

INGREDIENTS

- 2 (60 g) scoops chocolate ice cream
- 3 shots (90 g) espresso
- 2 tablespoons (30 ml) hazelnut syrup
- 1 cup (250 ml) skim milk
- 10 ice cubes
- Whipped cream, to serve
- Chocolate syrup, to serve
- Chocolate shavings, to serve

METHOD

- Combine the chocolate ice cream, espresso, hazelnut syrup, milk, and ice cubes in blender. Process until smooth.
- Divide the blended coffee mixture among 2 chilled tall glasses.
- Top with some whipped cream and drizzle with chocolate syrup. Garnish with chocolate shavings.
- Serve and enjoy.

NUTRITIONAL INFORMATION

Energy	Fat	Carbohydrates	Protein	Sodium
325 kcal	19.8 g	29.6 g	8.1 g	132 mg

ALMOND MOCHA FRAPPE

Preparation Time	Total Time	Yield
5 minutes	5 minutes	2 servings

INGREDIENTS

- 3 shots (90 ml) espresso
- 1/4 cup (80 ml) chocolate syrup
- 1 cup (250 ml) almond milk
- 10 ice cubes
- Whipped cream, to serve
- Chocolate syrup, to serve
- Chocolate shavings, to serve

METHOD

- In a high-speed blender, combine the espresso, chocolate syrup, almond milk, and ice. Process until smooth.
- Divide among 2 chilled glasses drizzled with some chocolate syrup on the sides. Top with some whipped cream, chocolate syrup, and chocolate shavings.
- Serve immediately and enjoy.

NUTRITIONAL INFORMATION

Energy	Fat	Carbohydrates	Protein	Sodium
224 kcal	2.9 g	51.1 g	2.8 g	303 mg

SOY COFFEE CRUMBLE FRAPPE

Preparation Time	Total Time	Yield
5 minutes	5 minutes	2 servings

INGREDIENTS

- 1 cup (250 ml) soy milk, unsweetened
- 1 cup (250 ml) strong brewed coffee
- 1/4 cup (30 g) cashew nuts
- 1/4 cup (30 g) cacao nibs
- 2 Tbsp. (40 ml) sugar-free syrup
- 10 ice cubes

METHOD

- Combine the soy milk, brewed coffee, cashew nuts, cacao nibs, sugar-free syrup, and ice in a blender. Process to desired consistency.
- Divide among 2 chilled tall glasses. Add some cacao nibs on top if desired.
- Serve and enjoy.

NUTRITIONAL INFORMATION

Energy	Fat	Carbohydrates	Protein	Sodium
255 kcal	6.4 g	40.1 g	8.1 g	105 mg

DARK MOCHA MILKSHAKE

Preparation Time	Total Time	Yield
5 minutes	5 minutes	2 servings

INGREDIENTS

- 3 shots (90 ml) espresso
- 2 (60 g) scoops chocolate ice cream
- 1 cup (250 ml) skim milk
- 3 Tbsp. (60 ml) dark chocolate syrup, plus more to serve
- 10 ice cubes
- Whipped cream, to serve
- Chocolate syrup, to serve

METHOD

- In a high-speed blender, combine the espresso, ice cream, skim milk, dark chocolate syrup, and ice cubes. Process until smooth
- Divide among 2 chilled glasses. Top with some whipped cream and then drizzle with chocolate syrup.
- Serve immediately and enjoy.

NUTRITIONAL INFORMATION

Energy	Fat	Carbohydrates	Protein	Sodium
311 kcal	6.9 g	41.1 g	7.8 g	203 mg

CHILLED TIRAMISU SHAKE

Preparation Time	Total Time	Yield
5 minutes	5 minutes	2 servings

INGREDIENTS

- 1 cup (250 ml) almond milk
- 1 tablespoon (7 g) unsweetened cocoa powder, dissolved in 2 Tbsp. hot water
- 1/4 cup (60 g) cream cheese
- 1 ½ cups (125 ml) strong brewed coffee, cooled
- 1/4 cup (80 ml) chocolate syrup
- 1/4 teaspoon (1.5 ml) vanilla extract
- 1/4 teaspoon (1.5 ml) orange extract
- 10 ice cubes
- Whipped cream, to serve

METHOD

- Combine the almond milk, cocoa powder, cream cheese, brewed coffee, chocolate syrup, vanilla extract, orange extract, and ice cubes in a blender. Process to desired consistency.
- Divide among 2 chilled glasses. Top with some whipped cream and then drizzle with chocolate syrup or sprinkle with cocoa powder.
- Serve and enjoy.

NUTRITIONAL INFORMATION

Energy	Fat	Carbohydrates	Protein	Sodium
313 kcal	16.8 g	37.7 g	8.8 g	196 mg

COFFEE APPLE CARAMEL COOLER

Preparation Time	Total Time	Yield
5 minutes	5 minutes	1 serving

INGREDIENTS

- 1 shot (30 ml) espresso
- 1/2 cup (125 ml) milk
- 1/4 cup (60 g) applesauce
- 2 Tbsp. (40 ml) caramel sauce
- 1 Tbsp. (15 ml) apple juice concentrate
- 5-6 ice cubes
- Whipped cream or vanilla ice cream, to serve
- Caramel sauce, to serve

METHOD

- Combine the espresso, milk, applesauce, caramel sauce, apple juice concentrate, and ice cubes in a high-speed blender. Process until smooth.
- Pour the blended coffee mixture into a chilled glass. Top with some whipped cream or ice cream and then drizzle with caramel sauce.
- Serve and enjoy.

NUTRITIONAL INFORMATION

Energy	Fat	Carbohydrates	Protein	Sodium
305 kcal	11.9 g	46.6 g	5.3 g	222 mg

PEANUT BUTTER COFFEE FRAPPE

Preparation Time	Total Time	Yield
5 minutes	5 minutes	2 servings

INGREDIENTS

- 3 shots (90 ml) espresso
- 1 cup (250 ml) almond milk, unsweetened
- 4 Tbsp. (80 g) peanut butter
- 2 Tbsp. (40 ml) caramel sauce
- 10 ice cubes
- Whipped cream, to serve
- Cacao nibs, to serve
- Caramel sauce, to serve (optional)

METHOD

- In a high-speed blender, combine the espresso, almond milk, peanut butter, caramel sauce, and ice cubes. Process until smooth
- Divide among 2 chilled glasses. Top with some whipped cream and cacao nibs. Drizzle with caramel sauce if desired.
- Serve immediately and enjoy.

NUTRITIONAL INFORMATION

Energy	Fat	Carbohydrates	Protein	Sodium
357 kcal	18.6 g	40.3 g	8.9 g	255 mg

MINTY WHITE MOCHA FRAPPE

Preparation Time	Total Time	Yield
5 minutes	5 minutes	2 servings

INGREDIENTS

- 3 shots (90 ml) espresso
- 1 cup (250 ml) skim milk
- 4 Tbsp. (80 ml) sugar-free white chocolate syrup
- 2 Tbsp. (40 ml) sugar-free peppermint syrup
- 10-12 ice cubes
- Whipped cream, to serve
- Cubed chocolate wafer bars, to serve

METHOD

- Combine the espresso, skim milk, white chocolate syrup, peppermint syrup, and ice cubes in a high-speed blender. Process until smooth.
- Divide among 2 chilled glasses. Top with some whipped cream and garnish with cubed chocolate wafer bars.
- Serve and enjoy.

NUTRITIONAL INFORMATION

Energy	Fat	Carbohydrates	Protein	Sodium
353 kcal	13.8 g	48.1 g	6.8 g	182 mg

MOCHA SHAKE WITH PEPPERMINT

Preparation Time	Total Time	Yield
5 minutes	5 minutes	2 servings

INGREDIENTS

- 3 shots (90 ml) espresso
- 1 cup (250 ml) milk
- 2 Tbsp. (40 ml) sugar-free chocolate syrup
- 2 Tbsp. (40 ml) sugar-free peppermint syrup
- 10 ice cubes
- Whipped cream, to serve
- Chocolate syrup, to serve

METHOD

- Combine the espresso, milk, chocolate syrup, peppermint syrup, and ice cubes in a high-speed blender. Process until smooth.
- Divide among 2 chilled glasses. Top with some whipped cream and then drizzle with chocolate syrup.
- Serve and enjoy.

NUTRITIONAL INFORMATION

Energy	Fat	Carbohydrates	Protein	Sodium
271 kcal	3.9 g	53.1 g	6.1 g	111 mg

ICED CHERRY COFFEE

Preparation Time	Total Time	Yield
5 minutes	5 minutes	1 serving

INGREDIENTS

- 2 shots (60 ml) espresso
- 1/2 cup (125 ml) milk
- 2 tablespoons (40 ml) sugar-free cherry syrup
- 5 ice cubes
- Whipped cream, to serve
- Chocolate syrup, to serve

METHOD

- Combine the espresso, milk, cherry syrup, and ice cubes in a shaker bottle. Cover with lid and shake well.
- Pour into a chilled glass. Top with some whipped cream and then add a drizzle of chocolate syrup.
- Serve and enjoy.

NUTRITIONAL INFORMATION

Energy	Fat	Carbohydrates	Protein	Sodium
339 kcal	13.9 g	46.1 g	7.8 g	126 mg

COFFEE MACADAMIA AND CARAMEL FRAPPE

Preparation Time	Total Time	Yield
5 minutes	5 minutes	2 servings

INGREDIENTS

- 3 shots (90 ml) espresso
- 1 cup (250 ml) skim milk
- 2 Tbsp. (40 ml) sugar-free macadamia syrup
- 2 Tbsp. (40 ml) sugar-free caramel syrup
- 10 ice cubes
- Caramel syrup, to serve

METHOD

- Combine the espresso, skim milk, macadamia syrup, caramel syrup, and ice cubes in a high-speed blender. Process until smooth.
- Divide among 2 chilled glasses. Drizzle with some caramel syrup on top.
- Serve and enjoy.

NUTRITIONAL INFORMATION

Energy	Fat	Carbohydrates	Protein	Sodium
271 kcal	3.9 g	53.1 g	6.1 g	111 mg

PUMPKIN MOCHA FRAPPE

Preparation Time	Total Time	Yield
5 minutes	5 minutes	2 servings

INGREDIENTS

- 1 cup (250 ml) strong brewed coffee
- 1/2 cup (125 g) pumpkin puree
- 2 Tbsp. (40 ml) sugar-free chocolate syrup
- 1/4 tsp. (1 g) pumpkin pie spice
- 1/2 cup (125 ml) almond milk, unsweetened
- 10 ice cubes
- Whipped cream, to serve
- Caramel syrup, to serve

METHOD

- Combine the brewed coffee, pumpkin puree, chocolate syrup, pumpkin pie spice, milk, and ice cubes together in a high-speed blender. Process until smooth.
- Divide among 2 chilled glasses. Top with some whipped cream and add a drizzle of caramel syrup.
- Serve and enjoy.

NUTRITIONAL INFORMATION

Energy	Fat	Carbohydrates	Protein	Sodium
280 kcal	2.7 g	35.2 g	8.1 g	168 mg

NUTELLA COFFEE FRAPPE

Preparation Time	Total Time	Yield
5 minutes	5 minutes	2 servings

INGREDIENTS

- 3 shots (90 ml) espresso
- 1 cup (250 ml) almond milk
- 3 Tbsp. (60 g) Nutella spread
- 2 Tbsp. (40 ml) sugar-free syrup
- 10 ice cubes
- Whipped cream, to serve
- Chocolate or caramel syrup, to serve

METHOD

- Combine the espresso, almond milk, Nutella, sugar-free syrup, and ice cubes in a high-speed blender. Process until smooth.
- Divide among 2 chilled glasses. Top with some whipped cream and then add a drizzle of chocolate or caramel syrup.
- Serve and enjoy.

NUTRITIONAL INFORMATION

Energy	Fat	Carbohydrates	Protein	Sodium
323 kcal	18.9 g	42.1 g	10.4 g	187 mg

COFFEE: IS IT GOOD OR BAD FOR YOU?

In previous years, there were discussions about the health effects of coffee.

Coffee, in general, can be a healthy beverage; but, it can also cause harm to the body when not taken properly. Now, let's take a closer look at the PROS and CONS of drinking coffee.

PROS:

1. Coffee like tea is an excellent source of antioxidants, which can help delay the signs of aging and protects the cells from harmful free-radicals.

2. Coffee without sugar and milk has a very minimal amount of calories. That is why it makes an excellent beverage for people who are watching their weight.

3. Coffee contains B-vitamins that can speed up your metabolism. This is beneficial for people trying to shed some weight because they get to burn more calories.

4. The caffeine in coffee acts as a stimulant that can increase brain activity and cognitive function.

5. Coffee can improve your mood, reduce fatigue, makes you more alert and physically active.

6. Since coffee can enhance brain function, researches show that people who drink coffee regularly have a reduced risk of Alzheimer's disease, dementia, and

Parkinson's disease when they reach old age.

7. Many studies also show that coffee drinkers have a lower risk of developing diabetes (type 2), liver cirrhosis, and liver cancer.

CONS:

1. Drinking too much coffee can cause anxiety, restlessness, irritability, jitteriness, panic attacks, and heart palpitations because of caffeine content. People who have a low tolerance to caffeine may also experience the same symptoms, so it is best to know your limits and listen to your body.

2. Drinking coffee towards the end of the day is not a good idea as it can disrupt sleep or reduce the quality of your sleep.

3. Drinking coffee is habit-forming. This is because caffeine is addictive. Withdrawal symptoms like irritability, lethargy, and headaches can occur when people regularly drink coffee and suddenly abstain from it.

Index

O

Orange-Kissed Black Coffee 2

P

Peanut Butter Coffee Frappe 68
Peppermint Black Coffee 6
Peppermint Mocha Frappe 43
Pumpkin Mocha Frappe 74

R

Raspberry Choco Coffee Shake 44
Raspberry Cream Coffee 29

S

Soy Coffee Crumble Frappe 62
Spiced Irish Cream Coffee Frappe 46
Spiced Mocha Shake 42
Sugar-Free Almond Coffee 39
Sweet Almond Coffee 16
Sweet Black Coffee Mexican-Style 8

Made in the USA
Middletown, DE
22 August 2023